HOW TO BEAT THE IRS, LEGALLY

I0453282

Dennis Noss, MSc. IRS Enrolled Agent

with Edward A. Lyon, JD

https://RetireBetterSooner.com

(650) 477-4370

Cayman Capital Management, Inc

https://CCMWealthStrategies.com

Registered Investment Advisor

Revision Publishing LLC books may be purchased for educational, business, or sales promotional use. For information, please email contact@revisionpub.com.

First Edition

How to Beat the IRS, Legally Library of Congress Control Number: 2025920167

ISBN 979-8-9929944-7-6

Cover/Interior Design by Samia Asif

Other books by Dennis Noss, MSc., E.A. and Edward A. Lyon, JD

Beyond 401(k): Retirement Security in an Insecure World

Contents

About the Authors

Dennis Noss, MSc. IRS Enrolled Agent

Dennis Noss has a Master of Science in Finance and Accounting from the University of Leicester in England and a Master of Public Health from Loma Linda University in California, where he studied epidemiology.

(Dr.) Dennis Noss is licensed and practiced as a podiatric physician and surgeon. He decided on a full-time career as a tax strategist and registered financial advisor when he was offered the opportunity to take over his family's financial advisory business over 20 years ago.

Dennis Noss is CEO of his own firm as a Retirement and Tax Strategist and is a securities-licensed registered investment advisor. He became certified professionally in retirement planning and in taxation as he feels the biggest threat to his client's future income has been inflation and taxation.

Dennis Noss specializes in custom-built tax-efficient asset and stock market portfolios with more safety, less volatility, have less expenses, can minimize and protect against loss, have higher rates of return and can amplify returns for maximized income, but also minimize or eliminate the tax.

Dennis Noss is a long-standing and current investment professional member of CFA Institute and has now been active in the financial industry for more than 20 years.

Dennis Noss is regulated as a fiduciary by the Department of Financial Oversight. As a fiduciary, it is his responsibility to strive to achieve the best results for his clients.

Dennis Noss is also federally licensed as an Enrolled Agent by the Department of the Treasury, with unlimited rights to practice before the IRS concerning all tax matters, including retirement plan actions, appeals and mediation.

Dennis Noss limits his tax practice to representation, individual and business tax planning, asset and investment tax planning strategies, and integrating financial services when appropriate. He does not do tax returns for clients and will refer you to a CPA or tax attorney if needed.

Dennis Noss is a past president of the IRS Enrolled Agent Society in San Jose, California. The license to practice as an Enrolled Agent is the highest credential issued by the Department of the Treasury to the IRS for competence in federal taxation. Some CPAs and attorneys also have this designation. Very few investment advisors also have this designation.

About the Co-Author

Edward A. Lyon, JD

Ed Lyon earned his bachelor's degree from Hamilton College and his JD from the University of Cincinnati College of Law, where he served as Executive Editor of the University of Cincinnati Law Review.

He has nearly three decades of experience in the tax and financial services industries, where he focuses on helping business owners take advantage of the tax code's legal "green lights" to pay less. He's the founder and CEO of the Tax Master Network, where he created the Tax Architect software program and helped train over 4,000 tax professionals across the country. He's currently the Chief Tax Planner for Excel Empire, where he created the Certified Tax and Business Advisor program.

Ed is the author of nearly a dozen books on taxes and tax planning. He writes two weekly tax columns for over 100,000 tax professionals and their clients, making him the most widely read tax strategist in the country. He's appeared on over 500 television and radio broadcasts, including CNN, Fox News, MSNBC, and CNBC.

Introduction

Are you satisfied with the taxes you pay?

Are you confident you're taking advantage of every available break?

Is your tax advisor giving you proactive advice to save on taxes?

If you're like most business owners, your answers are "no," "no," and "huh?" Maybe "LOL" to that last one.

And if that's the case, I've got bad news and I've got good news.

The bad news is, you're right. You *do* pay too much tax— maybe thousands more per year than the law requires.

You're almost certainly not taking advantage of every tax break you can. Our tax code is hundreds of pages long, with tens of thousands *more* pages of regulations. There are thousands more pages of IRS guidance, along with intimidatingly thick volumes of court cases interpreting all those laws, regulations, and guidance. The sad reality is, there's probably no one alive taking advantage of every tax break they're entitled to, simply because there are so many of them out there.

And most tax advisors aren't very proactive when it comes to saving their clients' money. Yes, they get the "right" numbers in the "right" boxes on the "right forms," and getting them filed by the "right" deadlines. But then they call it a day. They do a perfectly fine job recording the history you give them. But wouldn't you prefer someone to help you *write* your own history?

The good news is, you don't have to feel that way. You just need a better plan. And you've already taken a giant step in that direction, whether you realize it or not. Owning your own business is the biggest tax shelter left in America. Now you just need to take advantage of what you already have!

In this book, we're going to talk about some of the biggest mistakes that business owners make when it comes to their taxes. Then we're going to talk about how Excel Empire can help you solve those problems —legally, morally, and ethically.

I'm not here to make you an expert on taxes. Albert Einstein once said, "the hardest thing in the world to understand is the income tax," and if taxes were hard for the guy who came up with the theory of relativity, it's OK if they're hard for the rest of us. You'll see the word "generally" a lot in this book, because the concepts are more important than the details or the exceptions.

My goal here is to ask some pointed questions and get you to look at your taxes with a new eye. You make choices about your tax bill every day. Are you making the right choices? Or are you like most business owners and professionals, leaving money on the table, wasting money on taxes you just don't have to pay?

Supreme Court Justice Oliver Wendell Holmes once called taxes "the price we pay for civilization." But he never said we have to pay retail! And you certainly don't need to leave a tip. This book will help you start finding discounts throughout your return.

Failing to Plan

#1 Mistake: Failing to Plan

"There is nothing wrong with a strategy to avoid the payment of taxes. The Internal Revenue Code doesn't prevent that."

~William H. Rehnquist

The first mistake is the biggest mistake of all. It's failing to plan.

I don't care how good you and your tax preparer are with a stack of receipts on April 15. If you didn't know you could write off your kid's braces as a business expense, there's nothing we can do.

Remember the last time you drove a car? If you're like most people, you probably sat down in the driver's seat, strapped on your seat belt, turned the ignition, put the car in reverse, then backed your way to your destination, steering by what you could see out the rear-view mirror.

Wait a minute… you mean that's not how you do it?

Why Tax Planning

https://RetireBetterSooner.com

Well, that's how most tax preparers work. They spend lots of time looking back at what you did last year. But they don't spend much time looking forward. They can tell you all about what you did yesterday. But they don't tell you what you should do today to make tomorrow's return less painful.

Tax planning, on the other hand, gives business owners like you two powerful benefits you can't get anywhere.

First, it's the key to your financial defense. As a business owner, you have two ways to put cash in your pocket. There's financial offense, which means making more. And there's financial defense, which means spending less. For most of you reading this book, spending less is easier than making more. If you're a football fan, you've probably heard the saying, "Offense sells tickets. Defense wins games." Tax planning isn't as flashy as a Hail Mary touchdown. But it's exactly the sort of financial defense that wins games.

And for most of you reading this book, taxes are your biggest expense. So it makes sense to focus your financial defense where you spend the most. Sure, you can save 15% on car insurance by switching to GEICO.

But how much will that really save in the long run?

Second, tax planning guarantees results. You can spend all sorts of time, effort, and money promoting your business, and still not guarantee results. Or you can set up a medical expense reimbursement plan, deduct the cost of your teenage daughter's braces, and guarantee savings.

But those guaranteed results start with planning. You can't ever deduct money you spend on a medical expense reimbursement plan if you don't set it up in the first place.

Now that you understand why planning is so important, let's take a quick look at how the tax system works. This will "lay a foundation" for understanding the specific strategies we'll be talking about soon.

There's a popular myth going around that the Internal Revenue Code is 70,000 pages. That's a bit of an exaggeration. The "code" itself, as authorized by Congress and signed by various presidents over the years, fits in just under 600 pages. (You can order it from Amazon, if you have trouble sleeping and don't want to risk getting addicted to tranquilizers.) But throw in all the Treasury regulations, IRS pronouncements and publications, and you'll scream through 70,000 pages fast.

Of course, as every lawyer learns on Day One of law school, the law isn't what the law says it is—the law is what a judge says it is. So, throw in an entire library of Tax Court decisions, along with appeals of those decisions and even a handful of Supreme Court cases addressing tax questions, and you've got a byzantine mess on your hands. (What did the Byzantines do to get such a bad rap, anyway?)

Fortunately, you don't have to be a lawyer to understand the fundamental concept—and how Excel Empire can put it to work for you instead of against you. Here's the key to understanding code. Think of it as a series of red lights and green lights. The red lights are where you stop and pay tax. The green lights are where you go without paying tax.

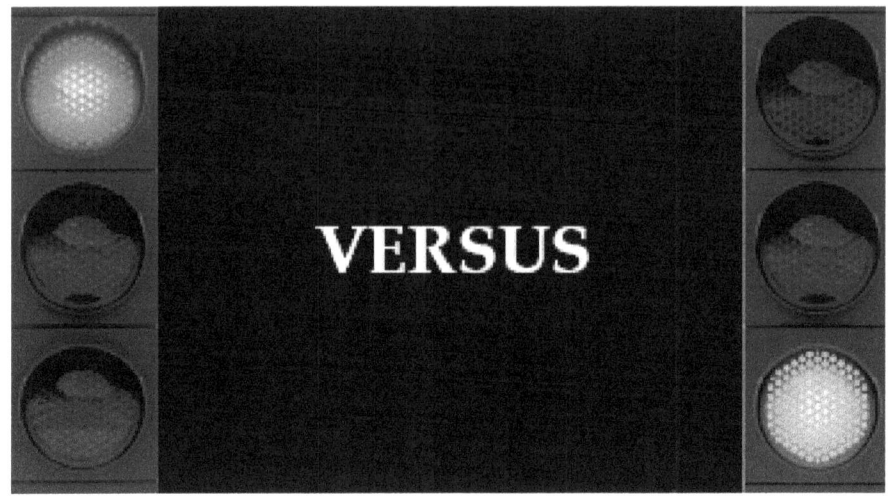

VERSUS

Red lights, green lights. Easy enough for a kindergartner, right?

Let's take a look at the red lights first. The big one is Code Section 61(a), which gives us the core definition of "gross income" that everything else flows from:

(A) General Definition

Except as otherwise provided in this subtitle, gross income means all income from whatever source derived, including (but not limited to) the following items:

1. *Compensation for services, including fees, commissions, fringe benefits, and similar items;*

2. *Gross income derived from business;*

3. *Gains derived from dealings in property;*

4. *Interest;*

5. *Rents;*

6. *Royalties;*

7. *Dividends;*

8. *Annuities;*

9. *Income from life insurance and endowment contracts;*

10. *Pensions;*

11. *Income from discharge of indebtedness;*

12. *Distributive share of partnership gross income;*

13. *Income in respect of a decedent; and*

14. *Income from an interest in an estate or trust.*

That's a pretty exhaustive list! But it's also pretty straightforward. The key words here are "whatever source derived, including (but not limited to)." In other words, *everything* falls into "gross income" *unless* it's specifically excluded.

Read between the lines and you'll discover that even illegal income is taxable. It's clearly "gross income derived from business." It's just not *legal* business. The IRS doesn't care how you make it; they just want their share! The good news, if you're operating most illegal businesses, is that you can deduct the same expenses as if you were running a legitimate business. For example, if you're a bookie, you can deduct the cost of a cell phone you use to take bets and mileage down to Smitty's Bar to collect envelopes. The only exceptions include expenses "contrary to public policy" (like whacking a rival over a territorial dispute) and most businesses involving drugs that are illegal at the federal level.

The next big red light comes right up front: Code Section 1:

(A) Married Individuals Filing Joint Returns And Surviving Spouses

There is hereby imposed on the taxable income of—

1. *every married individual (as defined in section 7703) who makes a single return jointly with his spouse under section 6013, and*

2. *every surviving spouse (as defined in section 2(a)), a tax determined in accordance with [the table of tax brackets]:*

Section 1 is also pretty straightforward. Here are the progressive tax rates you apply to your taxable income to calculate your actual bill.

There really aren't a lot of red lights left—probably less than you expect:

- Section 11 imposes tax the corporate income tax.

- Section 55 imposes the alternative minimum tax.

- Sections 3101 and 3111 impose FICA taxes on employees and employers.

- Section 1401 imposes self-employment tax on income from proprietorships and partnerships.

- Section 1411 imposes the net investment income tax.

But then the code starts laying out the *green* lights. That's where the fun starts! As former Senator Warren Magnuson once said, "The first 9 pages of the Internal Revenue Code define income; the remaining 1,100 spin the web of exceptions and preferences."

- Section 105(b) says that gross income doesn't include amounts "paid, directly or indirectly, to the taxpayer to reimburse the taxpayer for expenses incurred by him for the (as defined in section 213(d)) of the taxpayer, his spouse, his dependents (as defined in section 152, determined without regard to subsections (b)(1), (b)(2), and (d)(1)(B) thereof), and any child (as defined in section 152(f)(1)) of the taxpayer who as of the end of the taxable year has not attained age 27." Parse through the legalese, and you'll see that medical expense reimbursement plan benefits aren't taxable.

- Section 162(a) says," There shall be allowed as a deduction all the ordinary and necessary expenses paid or incurred during that taxable year in carrying on any trade or business"

- Code section 170 says, "There shall be allowed as a deduction any charitable contribution (as defined in subsection (c)) payment of which is made in the calendar year."

The list goes on and on and on and on and on.

Here's the bottom line. Most tax pros do a perfectly good job steering you through the red lights. And that's important! Blowing through the red lights is what gets you in trouble! But they either don't have the time, or the training, or the inclination to look more than superficially for the green lights. They tell you how much you owe, which is what you need. But they don't tell you how to pay less, which is what you really want.

Here's one final consideration before we finish up with red lights and green lights. In all 50 states, you can turn right on red so long as it's not prohibited at that particular intersection. The same is sometimes the case with taxes.

For example, if you go to your CPA and ask if you can put $30,000 in your Roth IRA, he'll tell you the Roth contribution is just $7,000. He might also tell you your income is too high to contribute to a Roth at all. That's a red light!

But . . . maybe you can contribute $30,000 to a SEP-IRA, deduct that contribution, then immediately convert that SEP- IRA to a Roth. It's not the same green light as putting $30,000 directly into the Roth. But it gets you the same place, by turning right on red.

Want to know if you've got a red-light CPA? Ask yourself this: when was the last time they came to you with an idea to save money? If the answer is "never," you've got a red-light CPA—and you're probably paying too much.

Now that you understand how the tax system works, let's take a closer look at how you calculate your tax bill—and how the red lights and green lights shape that process.

How to Calculate Your Tax

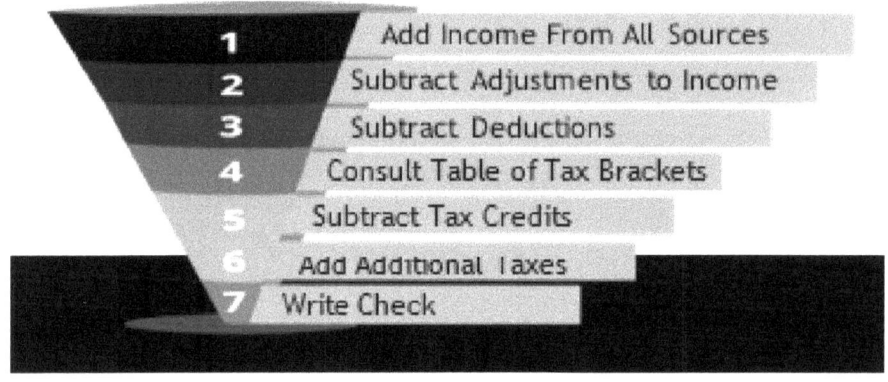

- The process starts by adding up your income from all sources to calculate "total income."

- Next, you'll subtract a set of specific "adjustments to income" that are available to all taxpayers, whether you itemize or not.

https://RetireBetterSooner.com

- Next, you'll deduct your standard deduction or total itemized deductions, whichever amount is greater.

- Next, you'll consult the table of tax brackets to determine your actual tax.

- Next, you'll subtract any available tax credits.

- Next, you'll add any extra taxes like self-employment tax or net investment income tax.

- Finally, you'll stroke a check to the IRS. If you've done a decent job with your withholding and quarterly estimates, you'll get a small refund. If you've done a *great* job, you won't owe anything or get anything back.

Gross Income Defined

1. Wages, salaries, tips, etc.
2. Business profits
3. Rents & royalties
4. Pension/401(k)/IRA
5. Interest, dividends, cap gains
6. Gambling & alimony
7. Illegal income

We've already discussed what counts as "gross income" when we covered red lights and green lights. What you need to understand here is that your goal should be to keep as much as possible off that taxable list. You want to pull income out of your business in the form of nontaxable employee benefits, rather than "compensation for services," "gross income derived from business," or "distributive share of partnership income." How? By converting them into things like nontaxable fringe benefits, retirement plan contributions, and the like.

Adjustments to Income

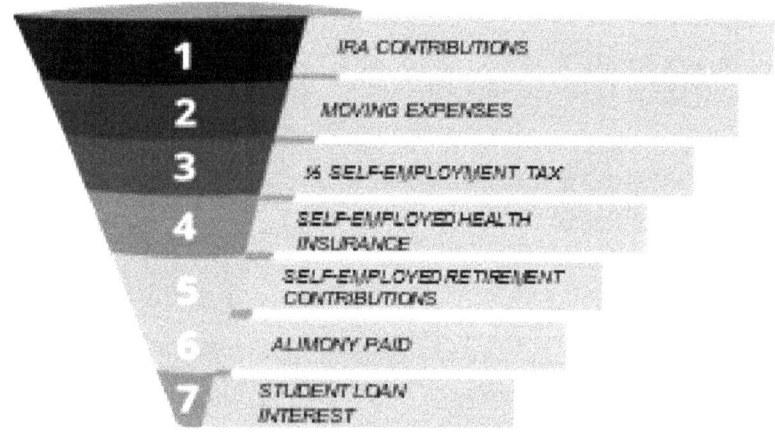

1. IRA CONTRIBUTIONS
2. MOVING EXPENSES
3. ½ SELF-EMPLOYMENT TAX
4. SELF-EMPLOYED HEALTH INSURANCE
5. SELF-EMPLOYED RETIREMENT CONTRIBUTIONS
6. ALIMONY PAID
7. STUDENT LOAN INTEREST

Once you've added up total income, it's time to start subtracting "adjustments to income." This is a group of specific green lights, listed on the first page of Form 1040, that you can take whether you itemize deductions or not. They include:

- IRA contributions,
- Moving expenses for active-duty military personnel,
- ½ of any self-employment tax you pay,
- Self-employed health insurance premiums you pay,
- IRA and self-employed qualified retirement plan contributions,
- Alimony payments (for agreements entered into *before* January 1, 2019),
- Student loan interest up to $2,500, and
- Charitable gifts up to $300 ($600 for joint filers) if you don't itemize deductions.

Total income minus adjustments to income equals "adjusted gross income," or AGI. These are also called "above the line" deductions, because you take them "above" the line that separates total income from AGI.

Once you've totaled your adjusted gross income, it's time to take your standard deduction or itemized deductions, whichever is more. For 2025, those amounts are $15,000 for singles, $22,500 for heads of households, $30,000 for married couples filing jointly, and $15,000 for married individuals filing separately. And here's the first real change that most people have seen after the Tax Cuts and Jobs Act of 2017. Standard deductions nearly doubled. Those amounts were already high enough that about 2/3rds of taxpayers already take them. The new rules have raised that number to nearly 90%.

Itemized Deductions

1. MEDICAL/DENTAL
2. STATE/LOCAL TAXES
3. FOREIGN TAXES
4. INTEREST
5. CASUALTY/THEFT LOSSES
6. CHARITABLE GIFTS
7. MISCELLANEOUS

If you're one of the remaining minority who benefit from itemizing, those green lights include:

- Medical expenses (but only to the extent they top 7.5% of your AGI),

- State and local income, sales, and property taxes paid (up to a total of $10,000 per year, which was a new limit for 2018),

- Foreign taxes paid, Mortgage interest on up to $1 million for loans closed before December 15, 2017, or $750,000 for loans closed after that date,

- Casualty and theft losses incurred as a result of a federally declared disaster, to the extent they exceed 10% of your AGI, and

- Charitable gifts.

Before the Tax Cuts and Jobs Act of 2017, you could write off a category of green lights called "miscellaneous itemized deductions"—at least to the extent they exceeded 2% of your adjusted gross income. These included employee business expenses, tax prep fees, and investment expenses. Those deductions are now eliminated. You could also write off interest on up to $100,000 of home equity interest you used for any purpose. That deduction is also zapped.

Finally, if you run a business taxed as a pass-through entity—a sole proprietorship, a partnership or LLC taxed as a partnership, or an S corporation or LLC taxed as an S corporation—you may or may not get a deduction for something called "qualified business income." (We'll discuss this in Chapter Four.)

Once you've subtracted your standard or itemized deductions, along with any qualified business income, you'll be left with "taxable income." At that point, you'll consult the table of tax brackets to see how much to pay.

Before the 2017 act, there were seven brackets, starting at 10%, and rising to 39.6% on income over about a half a million dollars. Some people actually paid more than that 39.6% top rate if they owed employment tax or net investment income tax on top of their regular income tax.

Tax Brackets: 2025		
Rate	Single	Joint
10%	0	0
12%	11,925	23,850
22%	48,476	96,950
24%	103,351	206,700
32%	197,301	394,601
35%	250,526	501,051
37%	626,351	751,601

And here's what those tax brackets look like for 2025. The Tax Cuts and Jobs Act keeps that same seven-bracket structure we had before, but shaves most of the actual rates by a couple of percent or so.

Tax Rates Through History

37% may sound like a pretty high top marginal rate, especially considering that it was just 35% until 2013. But today's rates are actually low by historical standards. The very first income tax, in 1913, had a top rate of just 5% on income over $500,000 – that's about $12.6 million in today's dollars. But rates shot up quickly to pay for World War I, then went even higher to pay for World War II.

The changes in tax brackets are pretty obvious. But here's another important change that you won't see reflected on the chart. It's become even more important since inflation rose after Covid. In 1985, Washington started indexing specific elements like standard deductions, personal exemptions, and tax brackets so that rising inflation wouldn't push taxpayers into higher brackets.

The IRS has traditionally used the Consumer Price Index, or CPI, to measure inflation. However, the new law specifies a different index, called the "chained" consumer price index. This index assumes that as prices go up, consumers react by choosing cheaper goods. For example, if the price of apples goes up, you probably won't stop eating them—but you might switch from Golden Delicious to Granny Smith. (If you're a millennial, substitute "avocado toast" for apples, and you'll get the point.)

The bottom-line result here is that that "chained" CPI rises more slowly compared to the regular CPI. The nonpartisan Tax Policy Center estimates that changing to chained CPI would increase taxes paid by 30% of the bottom quintile of the income distribution, 70% of the next quintile, and nearly all of the taxpayers in the top 60% of income. Bottom line, switching to chained CPI will function like a small but noticeable annual, across-the-board tax hike.

Tax Credits

1 FAMILY CREDITS

2 EDUCATION CREDITS

3 FOREIGN TAX CREDIT

4 GENERAL BUSINESS CREDITS

5 REAL ESTATE CREDITS

Finally, you'll subtract any available tax credits. These are dollar-for-dollar tax reductions, regardless of your tax bracket. So if you're in the 15% bracket, a dollar's worth of tax credit cuts your tax by a full dollar. If you're in the 35% bracket, an extra dollar's worth of tax credit cuts your tax by the same dollar.

There's no real secret to using tax credits, other than knowing what's out there. There are dozens available, but they fall into five main categories:

- Family-based credits, like the Child Tax Credit and Dependent Care Credit,
- Education credits, like the American Opportunity Credit and Lifetime Learning Credit,
- Foreign tax credits for taxes you pay to foreign countries,
- General business credits for all sorts of business expenses, like research & development, hiring employees from disadvantaged groups, pension plan startup expenses, and the like, and
- Real estate-based credits, like the low-income housing credit and renovation credit.

The biggest changes in the tax credit category under the Tax Cuts and Jobs Act of 2017 involves the Child Tax Credit. Under the old rules, it was capped at $1,000 per child, up to age 16. The credit phased out by $50 for each $1,000 of "modified adjusted gross income" above $75,000 (single filers) or $110,000 (joint filers). (Modified adjusted gross income equals regular adjusted gross income, plus a seemingly random laundry list of items like nontaxable municipal bond interest, student loan interest, half of your self-employment tax, and any deductible college expenses.) If the credit was more than your actual tax bill, you might qualify for an "additional child tax credit" to the extent of any earned income above $3,000. (Sure makes you wish you could fill out your taxes on a postcard, right?)

The 2017 law doubled the child tax credit to $2,000 per child. It raises the threshold for phasing it out to $200,000 for single filers and $400,000 for joint filers. It raises the age limit to for eligible children to 17. And it raises the refundable portion to $1,400, then indexes *that* amount for inflation.

Remember when we talked about those disappearing personal exemptions? The worst-hit taxpayers are the those with multiple children who lost the benefit of their personal exemptions. The new child tax credit rules should restore some of those lost benefits for those particular taxpayers.

The new law also provides a new $500 nonrefundable credit for dependents other than children. The rules here for claiming the credit are generally the same as they would be for claiming someone as a dependent.

But Wait . . . There's More!

1. SELF-EMPLOYMENT TAX
2. NET INVESTMENT INCOME TAX
3. ALTERNATIVE MINIMUM TAX
4. NANNY TAX

We're not done yet! As the television infomercials say, "But wait . . . There's more!"

You may also owe self-employment tax, which replaces Social Security and Medicare taxes for sole proprietors, partnerships, and LLCs.

There's also a 3.8% net investment income tax on investment income, which "Obamacare" introduced in 2013. This tax hits single taxpayers earning more than $200,000 and joint filers earning more than $250,000. For purposes of this rule, "investment income" includes interest, dividends, capital gains, rental income, royalties, and annuity distributions.

Then there's "alternative minimum tax," or AMT, which requires you to throw out some of the most valuable deductions, like state and local income taxes, and recalculate your bill all over, using slightly lower rates but a bigger base. Which amount is higher, regular tax or AMT? Pay that one, thank you very much.

The 2017 reform raises the exemption amount below which you're not subject to the tax. It also increases the phaseout of those exemptions. While this isn't nearly as good as *eliminating* the whole ridiculous travesty, it's protected millions of filers from its reach.

Finally, if you have household employees, you may have to pay a so-called "nanny tax" on their earnings. That may not sound like a big deal now. But it's definitely a big deal if you want to serve in the president's cabinet.

The bottom line here is that "tax brackets" aren't as simple as they might appear. Your *actual* tax rate can be quite a bit higher than your nominal "tax bracket."

So that's how the system works. (Easy peasy, right?)

Let's throw one more kink into the mix. We've talked several times about how the 2017 act turned off some green lights in order to lower overall rates. That entire law "sunsets" after December 31, 2025. And *that*, in turn, means if Washington doesn't act, the system reverts back to what it looked like in 2017, with some adjustments made for inflation. The green lights that were cut at that time, like state and local taxes over $10,000, become deductible again. Tax brackets will rise to their 2017 levels, meaning we're back to a 39.6% top rate.

Audit Paranoia

The second biggest mistake is nearly as important as the first, and that's *fearing*, rather than *respecting*, the IRS. Many business owners are simply afraid to take deductions they deserve, for fear of raising the proverbial "red flag."

But what does the kind of tax planning we're talking about really do to your odds of being audited? The truth is, most experts say it pays to be aggressive. That's because overall audit odds are so low, that most legitimate deductions simply aren't likely to wave "red flags."

Audit rates peaked in 1972 at one in every 44 returns. But lately they've dropped to historic lows. For 2022, the overall audit rate was just one in every 200 returns. Roughly half of those centered on a single issue, the Earned Income Tax Credit for low-income working families. The rest focused mainly on small businesses, especially sole proprietorships – and industries like pizza parlors and coin-op laundromats, where there are significant opportunities to hide income and skim profits. In fact, the IRS publishes a whole series of audit guides you can download from their web site that tell you exactly what they're looking for when they audit you!

So, if you *do* get audited, what then? Well, if you've properly documented your legitimate deductions, there's little to fear. In fact, about 15% of audits actually result in refunds. (Another 20% result in no change either way.)

And if you lose? You'll get what the IRS calls a "deficiency notice,' which is simply a bill for more tax. If you still think you're right, you can appeal it to the IRS. If you don't like the result you get there, you can appeal to the U.S. Tax Court. There's even a "small claims" division for disputes under $50,000 where you can represent yourself. (Caution—just because you can represent yourself doesn't mean it's a good idea!)

Just how aggressive can you get before risking actual penalties (as opposed to merely paying more tax)? You can avoid accuracy-related penalties if you have a "reasonable" basis for taking a position on your return. Generally, this means your position has more than one chance in three of being accepted by the IRS. You can file Form 8275 or 8275- R to disclose positions you believe to be contrary to law or regulations. But some advisors recommend *not* filing them. Why volunteer information that can attract unwanted attention? (Think of this as the tax equivalent of calling in an airstrike on your own position.)

Are you worried about getting in *real* trouble, as in criminal prosecution? Don't. Seriously. For fiscal year 2022, the Service initiated just 2,550 criminal investigations. That's an almost unimaginably tiny fraction of the 240 million returns they collect in a year. Out of those investigations, most lead to prosecutions (IRS investigators don't actually prosecute; they turn that job over to the Department of Justice.) Nearly all of them result in convictions leading to sentencing—the Feds don't take you to court if they're not already pretty sure they can win.

In the end, the average American really has nothing to fear from the IRS Criminal Investigations unit. As far as most of us are concerned, the IRS is just the government's collection agency, nothing scarier. You've got to do something pretty outrageous to draw one of those 2,550 investigations.

Sometimes, just changing how you report an item can dramatically change your odds of getting audited. For 2022, the IRS audited around 2% of Schedule C businesses reporting gross income over $100,000. Yet for that same year, they audited just 0.2% of partnerships and S corporations, regardless of how much they made. That suggests you can cut your odds of being audited by over 80% just by reorganizing your business.

Here's the bottom line. You should never be afraid to take a legitimate deduction. And if your tax professional *does* recommend you shy away from taking advantage of a strategy you think you deserve, ask them to explain exactly *why* they say so. And don't be satisfied with a vague, cowardly reply that it will "raise a red flag." *Ask*. Why does taking that particular deduction raise a red flag? What exactly does it do to your odds of getting audited? What happens if you do get audited? How hard will it be to substantiate your deduction? And what's the worst-case scenario if you can't? Remember, it's *your* money on the table, not theirs.

Choosing the *Wrong* Strategies

Nobody likes paying tax. Everyone wants to pay less. That dynamic sometimes leads taxpayers astray. It's easy to lose perspective sometimes and let the tax tail wag the business and financial dog. You don't want to obsess over taxes to the point where you create bigger tax or nontax problems down the road. Generally, these mistakes fall into two categories:

- The first group includes strategies that may save now but actually cost you more down the road. (This is most common with IRA and retirement plan deferrals, and we'll discuss it more in Chapter Five.) There are also strategies that make sense for someone else, but not you. Maybe you hear about them from a golf partner, or cousin, or (God forbid) on TikTok. Regardless, while it's completely legitimate and appropriate for them, the disadvantages outweigh the up-front benefits for you.

- The second group includes strategies that are just plain *bad*. The fees are too high for the benefits you get, or the strategy is borderline impermissible, or it's just plain fraud.

Inappropriate Strategies

The tax and investment world is full of strategies that are great for *some* taxpayers. But unscrupulous promoters know that some clients will do almost anything to avoid the pain of taxes, and those promoters are perfectly willing to use that pain to push products and strategies that aren't ideal—or sometimes aren't even appropriate—for those particular clients. Typically, these trade some level of tax relief today for an even greater tax bill or investment risk down the road.

Let's say you're a 45-year-old middle manager at the local paper mill or auto-parts manufacturer. You've finally worked your way out of the cubicles and into a real office, just before you learn you're part of the latest "rightsizing." You're feeling a little spicy, and you sure don't want to go back to work for "the man"!

So now you're looking at buying a franchise and building a sandwich empire. You even have the cash to do it, in your 401(k). The only problem is, drawing the money out of the account will mean paying a hefty tax bill, plus a 10% penalty for the early withdrawal.

But there's an escape hatch—a tool that lets you get the money for the franchise out of the account without paying the tax or the penalty. It's called a Rollover for Business Startup, or ROBS. Briefly, it lets you establish a C corporation to operate the franchise, adopt a 401(k) plan for that corporation, roll your balance from your old employer's plan into your new C corporation's plan, use that money to buy stock in the C corporation, then finally use the money you've paid into that C corporation (in exchange for the stock) to finance the franchise. (We'll talk more about C corporations in the next chapter.)

That sounds like a great solution. You have a problem—you need money to start your new business. You have the money, but you can't use it without paying a huge tax bill. The ROBS lets you access the money without paying the tax bill. Everyone wins, right?

But here's the problem. The ROBS creates a bunch of new problems and dangers down the road. And in all too many cases, those new problems outweigh the benefit you get from solving the up-front tax problem:

- The ROBS has to operate as a bona fide retirement plan for all the company's employees, with all the technical requirements and red tape that a qualified plan requires. If the ROBS fails that challenge, it can be disqualified, and you can be forced to pay immediate tax on the entire account balance. Ouch!

- The new business has to operate as a C corporation. If it loses money up front, like many startups do, those losses are locked inside the corporation until it shows taxable income to offset. You can't use those losses to offset income from a spouse or another job. And if your new startup doesn't succeed, which is awfully common with new businesses, you'll never get to use those losses.

- You can draw income from the new business only in the form of salary (taxed at your top marginal rate and subject to FICA too), or dividends. Any dividends you pay to your qualified plan will eventually be subject to tax at ordinary income rates, meaning you lose the advantage of lower rates on qualified corporate dividends.

- If the business succeeds and you eventually sell it, the gains on that sale that would have been taxed at lower capital gains rates (if you hadn't used the ROBS) go back into your retirement plan to be taxed at higher ordinary income rates.

- You also lose the chance to benefit from stepped-up basis at death. (Well, your *heirs* do.)

- If the business eventually fails, as a majority of startups do, you can't take the capital loss because it's locked inside the retirement plan. Even worse, there goes your retirement nest egg!

Now, there are workarounds for some of those problems. For example, you could use Roth IRA/401(k) dollars to avoid the tax on capital gains when you sell the business. But that escape hatch actually narrows the universe of taxpayers who can benefit from the strategy.

So, what do you think? Yes, the ROBS can help you solve the problem of finding money to start your business. But it can actually cost you more than those savings down the road.

Illegitimate/Illegal Strategies

Finally, some strategies just sound too good to be true—and it turns out they are.

If you're like most business owners, you're not just worried about taxes. You're worried about lawsuits, from disgruntled customers, vendors, employers, or random pedestrians who slip and fall on your sidewalk.

So . . . what if there was a magic trust you could use to own your business that would bulletproof you from lawsuits. And what if that same trust could defer tax on all your capital gains, in perpetuity?

There's a vendor, who will remain as nameless as Lord Voldemort (oops, said it!) who offers just such a trust. They promote it as a copyrighted, irrevocable non-grantor spendthrift trust. The copyright means you can only get it from that vendor or its agents. "Irrevocable" means you can't dissolve the trust and take back what's inside. "Non-grantor" means the tax bill on trust income doesn't come back to you unless the trust specifically distributes it to you. And "spendthrift" means your creditors can't reach into the trust to take your stuff.

That sounds awfully attractive, right? Almost too good to be true. And of course, it is.

The trust vendors claim that it can take advantage of code section 643(b) to defer tax on capital gains, in perpetuity. So let's "go to the tape," as the sportscasters say, and see what it actually says:

(b) Income

For purposes of this subpart and subparts B, C, and D, the term "income", when not preceded by the words "taxable", "distributable net", "undistributed net", or "gross", means the amount of income of the estate or trust for the taxable year determined under the terms of the governing instrument and applicable local law. Items of gross income constituting extraordinary dividends or taxable stock dividends which the fiduciary, acting in good faith, determines to be allocable to corpus under the terms of the governing instrument and applicable local law shall not be considered income.

That second sentence sure sounds promising. Translated into plain English, it suggests that if your trustee characterizes your gains from the sale of your business or other property as "extraordinary income" and allocates it to principal, rather than income, voila— tax avoided!

But take a closer look at that first sentence, which greatly limits the second. "The term 'income,' *when not preceded* by the words 'taxable'', "distributable net", "undistributed net", or "gross", means . . . ." (Emphasis added.) In other words, the first sentence makes clear that the second sentence doesn't exclude "extraordinary dividends" from taxable income at all. (The technical explanation here is that 643(b) applies to something called "trust accounting income," not "taxable" income.)

And as it turns out, code section 641(a) is quite clear on how to treat taxable income:

(a) Application of Tax

The tax imposed by section 1(e) [which sets out tax rates on trust income] shall apply to the <u>taxable income</u> of estates or of any kind of property held in trust, including—

(4) <u>income</u> which, in the discretion of the fiduciary, may be either distributed to the beneficiaries or accumulated.

You can probably see, however, how attractive that section 643(b) sounds, and why someone with big gains from the sale of a business or appreciated real estate might pay as much as $100,000 for that trust. Sometimes, we believe things because we want to, and let those desires cloud our better judgment. When it comes to taxes, that can be an expensive mistake.

Wrong Business Entity

> C-Corp?

> S-Corp?

> Partnership?

> Proprietor?

The next expensive mistake is choosing the wrong business entity.

Most business owners start as sole proprietors, then, as they grow, establish a limited liability company or corporation to help protect them from business liability. But picking the right entity involves all sorts of tax considerations as well. And many business owners are operating with entities that may have been appropriate when they were established – but just don't work as effectively now.

There are four ways you can organize your business:

- A **proprietorship** is a business you operate yourself, in your own name or a trade name, with no partners or formal entity. You report income and expenses on your personal return and pay income and self- employment tax on your profits. These are generally best for startups and small businesses with no employees in industries with little legal liability.

- A partnership is an association of two or more partners. General partners run the business and remain liable for partnership debts. Limited partners invest capital, but don't actively manage the business and aren't liable for debts. The partnership files an informational return and passes income and expenses through to partners. General partner distributions are taxed as ordinary income and subject to self- employment tax; limited partnership distributions are taxed as "passive" income.

- A **C corporation** is a separate legal "person" organized under state law. Your liability for business debts is generally limited to your investment in the corporation. The corporation files its own return, pays tax on profits, and chooses whether or not to pay dividends. Your salary is subject to income and employment tax; dividends are taxed at preferential rates. These are generally best for owners who need limited liability and want the broadest range of benefits. However, the administrative costs and complexities are also the highest.

- An **S corporation** is a corporation that elects not to pay tax itself. Instead, it files an informational return and passes income and losses through to shareholders according to their ownership. Your salary is subject to income tax and employment tax (Social Security and Medicare); pass-through profits are subject to ordinary income but not employment tax. These are generally best for businesses whose owners are active in the business and don't need to accumulate capital for day-to-day operations.

Notice you don't see "LLC" in that list. A limited liability company (LLC) is an association of one or more "members" organized under state law. Your liability for business debts is limited to your investment in the company, and LLCs may offer the strongest asset protection of any entity. However, a limited liability company is *not* a distinct entity for tax purposes. Single-member LLCs are taxed as proprietors, unless you elect to be taxed as an S corporation or a C corporation. Multi-member LLCs are taxed as partnerships, unless you elect to be taxed as an S corporation or C corporation. This flexibility makes LLCs the entity of choice for many startup businesses.

I can't make you an expert in business entities, not in a book like this. But I do want to walk through one popular choice to illustrate how important this question can be.

If you operate your business as a sole proprietorship, or a single-member LLC taxed as a sole proprietorship, you may pay as much in self-employment tax as you do in income tax. If that's the case, you might consider setting up an S corporation to reduce that tax.

If you're taxed as a sole proprietor, you'll report your net income on Schedule C. You'll pay tax at whatever your personal rate is. But (for 2021), you'll also pay self- employment tax, of 15.3% on your first $176,100 of "net self-employment income" and 2.9% of anything above that. You're also subject to a 0.9% Medicare surtax on anything above $200,000 if you're single, $250,000 if you're married filing jointly, or $125,000 if you're married filing separately.

Sole Proprietorship

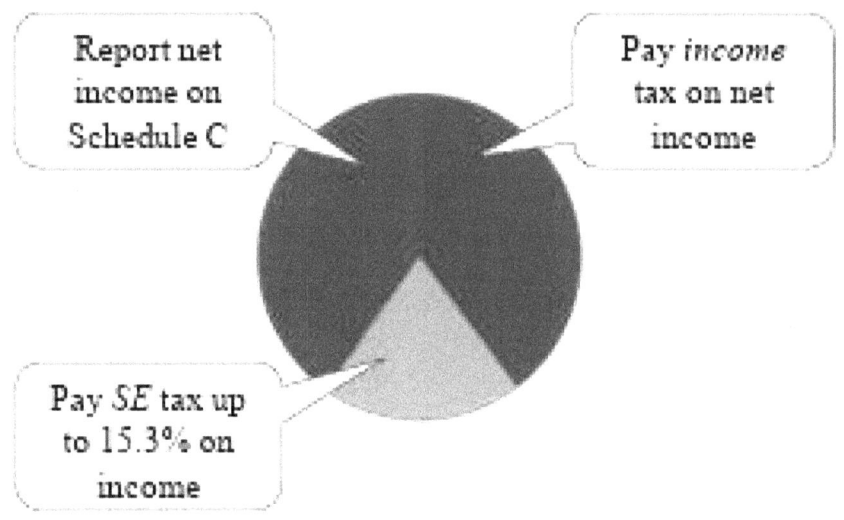

Report net income on Schedule C

Pay *income* tax on net income

Pay *SE* tax up to 15.3% on income

Let's say your profit at the end of the year is $80,000. You'll pay regular tax at your regular rate, whatever that is.

You'll also pay about $11,000 in self-employment tax.

That self-employment tax replaces the Social Security and Medicare tax that your employer would pay and withhold if you weren't self-employed. If you're like most readers, you're not planning to retire on that Social Security. You'll be delighted if it's all still there, but you're not actually counting on it in any meaningful way.

What if there was a way you could take part of that Social Security contribution and invest it yourself? Do you think you could earn more on your money yourself than you can with the Social Security Administration? Well, there is, and it's called an S corporation.

S-Corporation

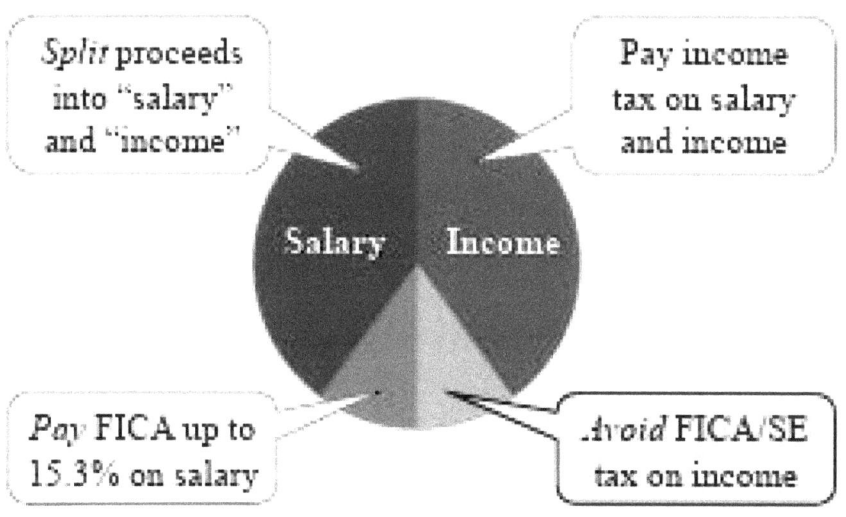

Split proceeds into "salary" and "income"

Pay income tax on salary and income

Salary Income

Pay FICA up to 15.3% on salary

Avoid FICA/SE tax on income

An S corporation is a special corporation that's taxed somewhat like a partnership. The corporation pays you a salary for the work you do. Then, if there's any profit left over, it passes the profit through to your personal return, and you pay the tax on that income on your own return. So the S corporation splits your income into two parts, wages and pass-through distributions.

Here's why the S corporation is so attractive. You'll pay the same 15.3% employment tax on your wages as you would on your self-employment income. (You'll also pay the extra 0.9% Medicare tax on self-employment income exceeding $200,000 or $250,000, depending on whether you file alone or jointly.)

BUT – there's no Social Security or self-employment tax due on the dividend pass-through. And that makes a world of difference.

Employment Tax Comparison

S-Corp FICA		Proprietorship SE	
Salary	$40,000	Income	$80,000
FICA	$6,120	SE Tax	$11,304
Net	$73,880	Net	$68,696

S-Corp Saves
$5,184

Let's say your S corporation earns the same $80,000 as your proprietorship. If you pay yourself $40,000 in wages, you'll pay about $6,120 in Social Security.

But you'll *avoid* employment tax on the income distribution.

And *that* saves you $5,184 in employment tax you would have paid without the S-corporation.

The best part here is that you just pay less tax. It's not like buying equipment at the end of the year to get big depreciation deductions. That may be a great strategy, but it also means spending something on the equipment to get that depreciation. It's not like locking money up into a retirement plan to get deductions. That may be another great strategy, but it also means you have to take money out of your budget to contribute to the plan.

As an S corporation shareholder-employee, you still have to pay yourself "reasonable compensation" for the service you provide as an employee—in other words, a credible equivalent to the salary you would have to pay to hire an employee to do the work for you. If you pay yourself nothing, or merely a token amount, the IRS can recharacterize up to all of your distributions as wage and hit you with some very hefty taxes, interest, and penalties. So don't get greedy! But according to IRS data, the average S corporation pays out about 40% of its income in the form of salary and 60% in the form of distributions. (And of course, we can help you calculate that amount.) So, you can see that there's at least a possibility for real savings.

Before we leave the subject of business entities, let's talk about the biggest change the Tax Cuts and Jobs Act of 2017 makes for most business owners: a new kind of income from pass-through businesses.

Some background: the tax code has always recognized that there are different kinds of income— and treated those kinds of income differently.

Ordinary income is what you earn from your work or your business. If you earn a salary from a job, and your spouse loses money in a business, you can net those amounts against each other. If you draw pension or IRA income, that's ordinary income too. Ordinary income is taxed at ordinary rates.

Investment income is income you earn from your portfolio. And some of it, like taxable interest income, is taxed at ordinary income rates. But different kinds of investment income can be taxed at different rates. Qualified corporate dividends, for example, are taxed at special rates and capped at 20%. Long-term capital gains from property held for more than a year are also capped at 20%. And investment income is subject to a 3.8% "net investment income tax" if your AGI exceeds $200,000 for single filers or $250,000 for joint filers.

Now, if you have capital losses in a year, you can subtract them from your capital gains. And you can subtract up to $3,000 of net capital losses against your ordinary income. But if your net capital loss is more than $3,000, you have to carry the remainder forward to future years. So, to at least that extent, investment income is walled off into its own little silo.

By the mid-1980s, taxpayers had figured a way around that wall. They discovered they could use borrowed money to increase their basis in investments like real estate, oil & gas, and equipment leasing, and write off huge paper losses, well in excess of what they had actually invested. They used those losses to offset their ordinary income from salaries and businesses, as well as investment income from their investment portfolios. That was great for taxpayers, of course, especially with marginal rates hitting 70%. But it wasn't so good for the U.S. Treasury.

So, in 1986, Congress created a new category of income, called passive income, from activities where you don't "materially participate." The 1986 rules said that you can write off passive losses against passive income – but not generally against ordinary income or investment income.

There's a rental real estate loss allowance for up to $25,000 of rental property losses, but *that* phases out starting at $100,000 of adjusted gross income. And so-called "real estate professionals" who qualify under special rules can deduct passive real estate losses against ordinary income. But for the most part, the 1986 rules walled off passive income and losses into a third silo.

Now Congress has created a fourth "silo," called qualified business income. Here's why they needed to do that. The Tax Cuts and Jobs Act lowered the top tax on C corporation income from 35% to 21%. That's a whole lot less than the maximum 37% tax on pass-through income from sole proprietorships, partnerships, and S corporations. To equalize the tax treatment between taxable and pass-through businesses, the Act defines the new qualified business income and lets you deduct 20% of that income, calculated on an activity-by-activity basis, from your taxable income for the year.

Qualified Business Income

QBI includes net business income from proprietorships, partnerships, and S corporations. It also includes pass-through income from real estate investment trusts, publicly traded partnerships, and qualified agricultural coops. But it doesn't include guaranteed payments you draw from your partnership or W-2 wages you draw from your S corporation. It also doesn't include investment income: most taxable dividends other than REITs, or coops, investment interest income, short-term or long-term capital gains, commodity or foreign currency gains, etc.

However, there are three important limits to this new deduction.

First, if your 2025 taxable income, *after* adjustments to income and itemized deductions, is over $197,300 ($394,600 for joint filers) your QBI deduction for each activity is limited to the greater of:

- 50% of the W-2 wages timely paid on behalf of that activity, *or*
- 25% of the W-2 wages plus 2.5% of the initial cost, immediately after acquisition, of all tangible property placed in service on behalf of that

activity. (Tangible property includes real estate, equipment and machinery, vehicles, or robots that replace your employees.) You can count the initial cost of the property towards this amount for 10 years.

Example: You own 20% of an S corporation that pays $500,000 in W2 wages and has $200,000 of property in service. Your QBI is the greater of $50,000 (50% of your 20% share of $500,000 in wages) or $26,000 (25% of your 20% share of $500,000 in wages plus 2.5% of your 20% share of the $200,000 in depreciable property).

This may mean that careful planning is required to maximize your deduction if your taxable income before subtracting QBI is enough to phase out the deduction.

Second, if your QBI comes from a "specified service business" (medicine, law, accounting, actuarial science, financial services, consulting, performing arts, athletics, or any business that relies on the "reputation or skill of one or more employees"), your deduction for that activity phases out as your taxable income rises from $197,300-247,300 (single filers) or $394,600-494,600 (joint filers).

This may mean that careful planning is required to define "specified service income" activities and segregate them from non-service activities in order to make the most of the opportunity. (In January 2019, the IRS issued final regulations offering more guidance in this area.)

Third, and finally, the overall QBI deduction is limited to 20% of your taxable income in any particular year.

(There's no provision for carrying over any unused deduction. However, if your QBI for the year is below zero, you can carry the loss forward to the next taxable year.)

The new rules immediately suggested several ways to maximize the new benefit. And while the IRS eventually issued regulations shooting many of them down, that hasn't stopped planners from working to maximize the new deduction. When critics of the tax bill said it would encourage "gaming the system," *this* was exactly the provision they were talking about. *This* was ground zero for the games.

Cut Taxable Income

If your taxable income is above the phase out threshold, consider strategies to intercept income before they reach your personal return. These might include shifting income to a C corporation or deferring income into a qualified retirement plan.

Create W-2 Income

If you currently operate a non-service business as a sole proprietor or partner, you have few or no W-2 employees, and your taxable income is above the threshold, consider establishing an S corporation and paying yourself a W-2 wage to create a base for taking advantage of the deduction.

"Cracking and Packing"

Consider "cracking and packing" strategies to avoid the limits on specified service income.

If your primary activity is a specified personal service, consider "cracking" out ancillary activities, like marketing or management, into a separate activity. You'll still lose out on the deduction for that primary service activity. But you'll preserve the deduction for the ancillary activities that don't fall under the service business definition. (The IRS has issued proposed regulations stating that a specified service business includes any trade or business that provides 80% or more of its property or services to a specified service business, as long as the two businesses share 50% or more common ownership.)

If a business earns less than 10% of its income from specified service *activity,* it won't be considered a specified service *business* for purposes of these new rules.

Segregate Real Estate

If you own real estate for your business to occupy, consider separating that real estate into a separate entity and paying it the highest reasonable rent to qualify for the deduction.

Contractors to Employees

If your business uses independent contractors, consider making them W-2 employees to maximize the W-2 base for calculating the QBI deduction. (Of course, if those contractors are also paying attention to the law, they may prefer to keep that status!)

Final Notes on QBI

This is going to sound self-serving. But this really isn't "do- it-yourself" planning. Just because you can buy a tool to do something yourself, instead of hiring a pro to use it, doesn't mean you *should*. If you go to Amazon and search for "orthopedic bone saw," you can find them for under twenty bucks. (Take a look. Seriously, it's terrifying!) But just because you can buy the tool, cheap, it doesn't mean you should be setting your kids' broken bones!

Want to hear something funny? Here's what the congressional conference committee responsible for final text of the QBI provisions said in their report:

> *"It is not anticipated that individuals will need to keep additional records due to the provision. It should not result in an increase in disputes with the IRS, nor will regulatory guidance be necessary to implement this decision."*

Ha! Do you think they actually *believed* that? Or is it just something they told themselves to feel better about unleashing a hurricane of new uncertainty into the system? How do you think they felt in January 2019, when the IRS issued *278 pages* of regulations interpreting the new provision?

Wrong Retirement Plan

Now let's talk about the fifth of our expensive mistakes: choosing the wrong retirement plan. As the chart below shows, the amount you can contribute at any income level varies widely according to which type of plan you have. If you make $100,000, for example, you can contribute

$25,000 to a simplified employee pension (SEP), $19,500 to a SIMPLE IRA, and $48,500 to a 401(k). (And that's before any catch-up contributions you can start making at age 50.) But contribution limits aren't all you need to know. Which plan gives you the best combination of contribution, flexibility, and liquidity?

Contribution by Income

■ SEP ■ SIMPLE ■ 401(k)

I'm not here to make you an expert on retirement plans. But I *can* help you decide pretty quickly if the plan you have is right for you – or if you should be looking for something more suited for your specific needs. So, bear with me, even if the next few pages look intimidating. These are some very powerful strategies.

We'll assume for the purposes of this discussion that you've already decided you want to save more than the $7,000 you can save in an IRA. We'll also assume, at least for the next few pages, that you want a "traditional" arrangement, where you deduct the contributions you make now and pay tax on withdrawals. (We'll address alternatives, including Roth arrangements and life insurance, towards the end of the chapter.)

Simplified Employee Pension

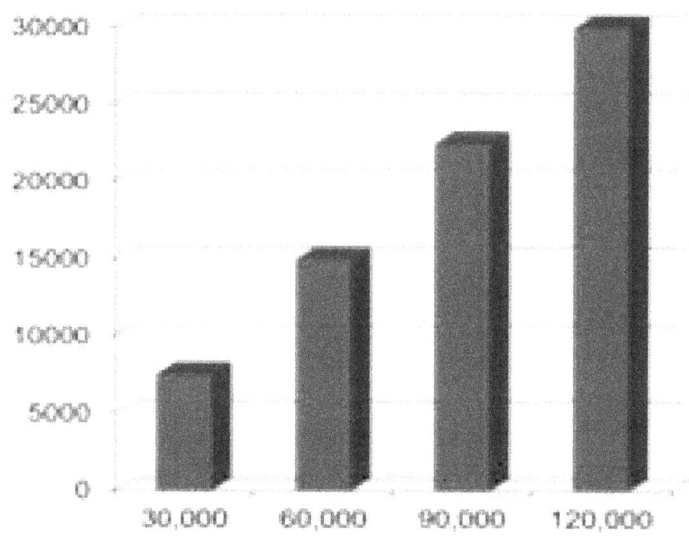

The Simplified Employee Pension, or "SEP," is the easiest plan to set up because it's just a turbocharged IRA:

- If you're self-employed, you can contribute up to 25% of your "net self-employment income."
- If your business is incorporated and you're salaried, you can contribute 25% of your

"covered compensation," which essentially means your salary.

- The maximum contribution for any single employee in 2025 is $70,000.

- If you've got employees, you'll have to contribute for them, too if they've reached age 21, worked for you for at least three of the five preceding years, and earned at least $750 in 2025. You generally have to contribute the same percentage for your employees as you do for yourself. However, if your income is significantly higher than that of your employees, you can use what's called an "integrated" formula to make extra contributions for higher income earners.

- The money goes straight into regular IRA accounts you set up for yourself and your employees. There's no annual administration or paperwork required.

- SEP assets accumulate tax-deferred over time. You'll pay tax on them at ordinary income rates when you withdraw them in retirement. There are penalties for early withdrawals before age

59½, and for failing to take required minimum distributions beginning at age 73.

The SEP is easy to adopt, easy to maintain, and flexible. If there's no money to contribute, you just don't contribute. But remember, the contribution is limited to a percentage of your covered compensation. So, for example, if you set up an S corporation to limit your self-employment tax, you'll also limit your SEP contribution because it's based on that lower salary amount.

SIMPLE IRA

The next step up the retirement plan ladder is the SIMPLE IRA. This is another "turbocharged" IRA that lets you contribute more than the usual $7,000 limit:

- You and your employees can "defer" and deduct 100% of your income up to $16,500.

- Those age 50 or older you can make an extra $3,500 "catch up" contribution.

- But—you have to match everyone's deferral or make profit-sharing contributions. You can match employee contributions dollar-for-dollar up to 3% of their pay or contribute 2% of everyone's pay whether they choose to defer or not. If you choose the match, you can reduce it as low as 1% for two years out of five.

- The money goes straight into employee IRAs. You can designate a single financial institution to hold the money, or let your employees choose where to hold those accounts.

- There's no set-up charge or annual administration fee for the plan. You're simply establishing special IRAs for your employees. You're not establishing a qualified plan trust to hold the assets like you would with a 401(k) or defined benefit plan.

- SIMPLE assets accumulate tax-deferred over time. You'll pay tax at ordinary income rates when you withdraw them in retirement. There are penalties for early withdrawals before age 59½ and failing to take required minimum distributions beginning at age 73.

The SIMPLE IRA may be best for part-time or sideline businesses earning less than $66,000, because the flat $16,500 contribution is higher than the 25% SEP contribution for incomes up to $66,000. And it may be best for lower-paid employees. The maximum contribution is below the $23,500 limit for a 401(k). But how many of your employees will actually contribute that maximum amount anyway?

401(k)

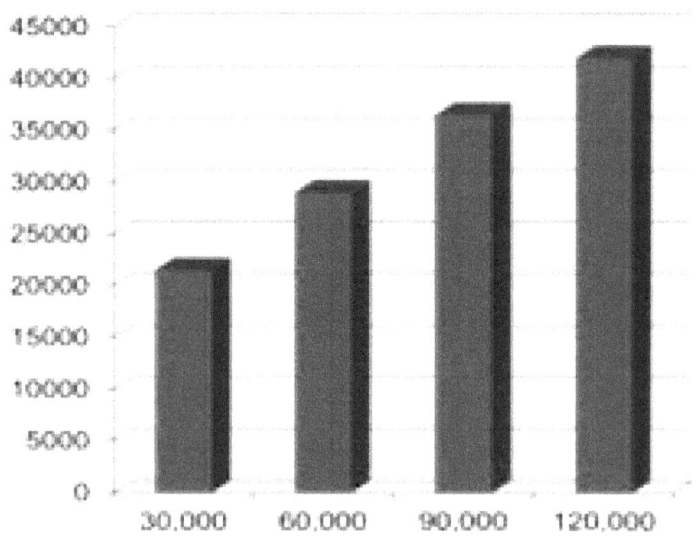

The next step up the retirement plan ladder is the 401(k).

Most people think of 401(k)s as retirement plans for bigger businesses. But you can set up a 401(k) for any size business. In fact, you can even set up what's called a "solo" or "individual" 401(k) just for yourself.

The 401(k) is a true "qualified" plan. This means you'll set up a trust, adopt a written plan agreement, and choose a trustee. But the 401(k) lets you contribute far more money, far more flexibly, than either the SEP or the SIMPLE.

- You and your employees can "defer" and deduct 100% of your income up to $23,500 for 2025. If you're 50 or older, you can make an extra $7,500 "catch up" contribution. At ages 60, 61, 62, and 63, that catch-up amount is $11,250.

- You can choose to match contributions or make "profit-sharing" contributions up to 25% of everyone's pay. (If you operate as an S corporation, you can contribute up to 25% of your salary, but not any pass-through distributions.) That's the same percentage you can save in your SEP – *on top of* the $23,500 deferral.

- The maximum contribution for 2025 is $70,000 per person, plus any "catch up" contributions.

- You can offer yourself and your employees plan loans, hardship withdrawals, and all the bells and whistles "the big boys" offer their employees.

- You can use "cross-testing" to skew profit-sharing contributions to certain employees. "Age-weighted" plans allocate more to older employees (on the theory that they have less time to save for retirement); "integrated" and "super-integrated" plans allocate more to higher-paid employees (on the theory that they get no benefit from Social Security for their income above the Social Security wage base); and "rate group" plans divide employees into groups (such as managers, administrators, and salespeople) and make different contributions for each group.

- 401(k) assets accumulate tax-deferred over time. You'll pay tax at ordinary rates when you withdraw them in retirement. There are penalties for early withdrawals before age 59½ and failing to take required minimum distributions beginning at 73.

The downside? 401(k)s are true "qualified" plans, which means more administration than SEPs or SIMPLEs. You'll have to file Form 5500 reporting contributions and assets, every year. And there are complicated anti-discrimination and "top-heavy" rules to keep you from stiffing your employees while you stuff your own account.

However, if the 401(k) really *does* make sense, there are three alternatives that might make administration easier:

- A "SIMPLE" 401(k) avoids nondiscrimination and top-heavy rules in exchange for guaranteed employer contributions. You and your employees can defer 25% of covered compensation up to the SIMPLE plan contribution limits. Your business has to contribute 2% of covered comp or match contributions up to 3% of covered comp. This works if you want a true 401(k), but you're afraid your employees won't contribute enough to let you make meaningful deferrals. You can also convert an existing 401(k) to a SIMPLE 401(k).

- A "Safe Harbor" 401(k) avoids nondiscrimination (but not top-heavy) rules in exchange for bigger employee contributions. You and your employees can defer up to the regular 401(k) limit. You can either: 1) contribute 3% of covered comp; or 2) match contributions dollar-for-dollar up to 3% of covered comp and fifty-cents-on-the-dollar for contributions between 3% and 5% of covered comp. You can even make extra profit-sharing contributions on top of the required contributions.

- If you operate your business all by yourself, with no employees other than your spouse, you can establish an "individual" 401(k) with less red tape.

Finally, if you want to contribute more than the $66,000 limit for SEPs or 401(k)s, you might consider a defined benefit plan. This is your father's retirement plan – the traditional "pension plan" that so many employers have stopped offering because they can't afford it anymore. However, it can still be a great choice for older, highly compensated business owners with few employees.

- Defined benefit plans let you guarantee up to $280,000 in annual income (2025 limit).

- You can contribute, and therefore deduct, as much as you need to finance that benefit. You'll calculate those contributions according to your age, your desired retirement age, your current income, and various actuarial factors.

- A "cash balance" plan lets you aim for a specified account balance at a specified retirement age, rather than a specified income throughout retirement. These are generally easier and less expensive to administer than a traditional full-blown defined benefit plan. They also let you invest part of your plan contributions in permanent life insurance, which can "complete" the plan for your family if you don't live long enough to fully fund it yourself.

- A 412(e) plan (previously called a 412(i) plan), is a defined benefit plan funded entirely with life insurance or annuities. Because those vehicles generally return less than a traditional securities portfolio, you can contribute (and deduct) even more while you're still working. The downside, of course, is that you're accepting a lower return than you might earn in equity markets. However, some conservative investors who feel uncomfortable investing in stocks are happy to take that deal.

The biggest problem with the defined benefit plan is the required annual contributions. If your business doesn't have the money, you still have to pay. However, you can combine a defined benefit plan with a 401(k) or SEP to give yourself a little more flexibility. Let's say you could contribute up to $100,000 to a defined benefit plan, but you're not confident you can commit to that much every year. You might set up a defined benefit plan with a $50,000 contribution, then pair it with 401(k) for another $50,000. If business is poor in a particular year, you can choose to skip the 401(k) that year.

So, now that we've covered the menu of traditional employer-sponsored retirement plans, let's throw another wrench into the mix. Do you even want or need a traditional plan? Or would you be better off with an alternative? Perhaps even giving up the current tax break?

All of the plans we've discussed so far assume that you're better off taking a tax deduction for plan contributions now, as they go in the plan, then letting plan assets accumulate tax-free over time, and then paying tax on withdrawals, at ordinary income rates, when you need them for retirement.

That's a great strategy if your tax rate is higher now than it will be in retirement. You benefit now by avoiding tax on contributions, which puts more to work for you today. And you benefit later by paying less tax on withdrawals.

But that traditional pattern doesn't always hold true. (Remember the graphic charting marginal tax rates we saw back in Chapter One?) Maybe you're young, just starting your career, and your income is low. Maybe you're transitioning from one career or business to another, and your income is temporarily low. Maybe you think that tax rates in general will rise. (Today's top marginal rate may seem high at 37%, but that's actually quite low by historical standards.) Sometimes, contributing to a traditional retirement plan creates a ticking tax time bomb and actually *costs* you money over the long run.

Here are two alternatives you might consider if standard qualified plans don't fit the bill:

- "Roth" accounts take the traditional defer-now, pay- later arrangement and turn it on its head. The basic Roth IRA doesn't give you any deduction for contributions you make today. But your withdrawals are generally tax-free so long as they've "aged" at least five years. Tax-free income sounds great, right? However, contributions are limited to $7,000 per year ($8,000 if you're 50 or older), and your contribution phases out beginning at incomes over $150,000 (single filers) or $236,000 (joint filers). (If your income is above those limits, you can still fund a Roth by contributing the maximum to a nondeductible traditional IRA, then immediately convert it to a Roth.)

If you sponsor a 401(k), you can choose to designate your salary deferrals up to $23,500 as "Roth" deferrals. You won't get any deduction today, but your withdrawals down the road will be tax-free. You can also choose to designate employer contributions for Roth treatment, too.

If you have a SEP, you can create a backdoor "Roth SEP" by making a deductible SEP contribution, then immediately converting it to a Roth. Roth conversions in general are a subject for another book—I just want you to be aware that the possibility exists. (You can make a similar move with a SIMPLE IRA, but you have to wait at least two years from the time you contribute the money until the time you convert it to a Roth. That also means paying tax on the first two years of growth on that contribution, too.)

- Permanent life insurance policies that include a cash value can offer several significant tax breaks for supplemental retirement savings. There's no deduction for premiums you pay into the contract. But policy cash values grow tax deferred. And you can take cash from your policy, tax-free, by withdrawing your original premiums and then borrowing against remaining cash values. You'll pay (nondeductible) interest on your loan, but you'll earn it back on your cash value. Many insurers offer "wash loan" provisions that let you borrow against your policy with little or no out-of-pocket costs.

These advantages aren't completely unlimited. If you stuff too much cash into the policy in the first seven years, it's considered a "modified endowment contract" and all withdrawals are taxed as ordinary income until you exhaust your inside buildup.

Insurers offer four main types of cash-value policies with four different investment profiles to suit different investors. The key is finding a policy that matches your tolerance for risk:

- ▶ "Whole life" resembles a bank CD in a tax-advantaged wrapper, with required annual premiums and strong guarantees. The best contemporary versions of this product includes paid-up additions and adds high cash value with increased flexibility.

- ▶ "Universal life" generally resembles a bond fund in a tax-advantaged wrapper, with flexible premiums but less strong guarantees. Some insurers also offer "indexed universal life," which lets you profit from equity markets but give you a guaranteed return even when those markets are down.

- ▶ "Variable life" lets you allocate cash values in a series of "subaccounts" resembling mutual funds with both the returns and losses of a typical mutual fund in a tax-deferred wrapper. You can choose "variable whole life" with required premiums and stronger guarantees, or "variable universal life" contracts with flexible premiums and less strong guarantees. There's also a "hybrid" version that acts like a collar on a market-based account, limiting your upside return and downside losses.

▶ "Index universal life" typically tracks an equity- based index and combines that with a guaranteed floor. This provides potential for higher gains based on the "crediting method" (which determines how much of the markets upside you get) and specific indexes chosen. In other words, when markets go up, you get part (but not all) of the upside – and when they go down, you get the guaranteed floor rate.

Once again, I'm not here to make you an expert in retirement plans or alternatives. My goal is simply to open your eyes to the wide variety of plans and options to alert you that the plan you have may not really be the right plan for you. I also protect you from the common trap of assuming that deferring today's income is always the right retirement planning strategy.

Missing Family Employment

- Ages 7+
- Standard deduction amount is tax-free
- Next block of income taxed at 10%
- "Reasonable" wages
- Written job description, timesheet, check
- Account in child's name

Now let's talk about the sixth mistake: missing family employment. Hiring your children and grandchildren can be a great way to cut taxes on your income by shifting it to someone who pays less.

- Yes, there's a minimum age. They have to be at least seven years old—at least according to a 1977 Tax Court decision. Some advisors recommend hiring younger children to model for your business's marketing; however, that strategy has not been tested in court.

- Their first $15,000 of earned income is taxed at zero. That's because $15,000 is the standard deduction for a single taxpayer – even if you claim them as your dependent. Their next $11,925 of taxable income is taxed at just 10%. That may be more income than you would have expected you would be able to shift downstream.

- You have to pay your child a "reasonable" wage for the service they perform. The Tax Court says this is what you'd pay a commercial vendor for the same service, with an adjustment made for the child's age and experience. So, if your 12-year-old cuts grass for your rental properties, pay him what a landscaper might charge. If your 15-year-old helps keep your books, pay him a bit less than a bookkeeping service might charge. Does anyone have a teenager who helps with your web site or social media marketing? What would you pay a commercial designer for that service? (The answer is: enough to make a nice difference in your tax bill!)

- To audit-proof your return, write out a job description and keep a timesheet of the work they do.

- Pay your child by check, so you can document the payment.

- You have to deposit the check into an account in the child's name. But it doesn't have to be his pizza-and- Nintendo fund. It can be a Section 529 college savings plan. Or it can be a custodial account that you control until they turn 21. Now, you can't use money in a custodial account for your obligations of parental support. But private and parochial school aren't obligations of parental support. Sleepaway summer camp isn't an obligation of parental support.

Let's say your teenage daughter wants to spend two weeks at horse camp. You can earn the fee yourself, pay tax on it, and pay for camp with after-tax dollars. Or you can pay her to work in your business, deposit the check in her custodial account, and then, as custodian, stroke the check to the camp. Hiring your daughter effectively lets you deduct her camp as a business expense.

Here's another little bonus you'll like. If you hire your child to work in an unincorporated business, you don't have to withhold for Social Security until they turn 18. So this really is tax-free money. You'll still have to jump through some paperwork hoops, like issuing a W-2 at the end of the year and reporting their income on their own return if the income is enough to require them to file themselves. But this is painless compared to the tax you'll waste if you don't take advantage of this strategy.

You can also use a child's income to open a Roth IRA. There's no requirement that you have to use the actual wages you pay them to fund the account – merely paying the wages is enough to qualify to open the account, and you can use any dollars to make the deposits. At a minimum, you'll give your child a decade or two of head start on retirement savings. Thanks to the miracle of compound interest, that could mean a six- or seven-figure advantage. Starting a Roth IRA also gives you a reason to start teaching your child about investing and markets that will give them a further financial advantage in adulthood.

Finally . . . just *maybe* . . . hiring your kids to work for you might teach them a thing or two about the value of a dollar in a world that seems more obsessed with money every single day. If you want to raise your children with sound values, you can't start the "money" discussion too soon!

Missing Medical Benefits

Now let's talk about health-care costs. Surveys used to show that taxes *used to be* small business owners' biggest concern. Now it's rising health care costs.

If you pay for your own health insurance, you can deduct it as an adjustment to income on Page 1 of Form 1040. If you itemize deductions, you can deduct unreimbursed medical and dental expenses on Schedule A, *if* they total more than 7.5% of your adjusted gross income. But most of us just don't spend that much on our healthcare. That means we lose thousands in otherwise legitimate deductions.

What if there was a way to write off medical bills as business expenses? There is, and it's called a Medical Expense Reimbursement Plan, or Section 105 Plan.

Owner Eligibility

Business Entity	How to Qualify
Proprietorship	Hire Spouse
Partnership	Hire Spouse (if <5% owner)
S-Corporation	>2% Shareholders ineligible
C-Corporation	Hire Self

The first thing you need to know about a MERP is that it's an *employee* benefit plan. That means (spoiler alert) it requires an employee:

- If your business is taxed as a sole proprietorship, you're considered self-employed. You can't establish the plan for yourself. However, if you're married, you can hire your spouse.

- If your business is taxed as a partnership, you're also considered self-employed. Again, you can't establish the plan for yourself. However, you can still hire your spouse so long as he or she owns less than 5% of the business.

- If your business is taxed as an S corporation, both you and your spouse are considered self-employed. This means you'll need another source of income, not taxed as an S corporation, to establish the plan. (Alternatively, you can establish a health savings account, which we'll discuss in a few pages, to give yourself most of the same benefit as the 105 plan.)

- If your business is taxed as a "C" corporation, you qualify as your own employee, so you can simply hire yourself.

If you're married, and you choose to hire your spouse, you don't even have to pay them a salary. You can compensate them in the form of benefits only, which avoids the hassle of filing payroll returns. The main requirement here is that the benefits you pay have to be "reasonable compensation" for the service they perform. If your spouse works an hour a month filing invoices for you, you'll probably have a hard time convincing an auditor that that's "reasonable" for $4,000 worth of LASIK surgery!

Eligible Expenses

- Major medical, LTC, Medicare, "Medigap" insurance
- Co-pays, deductibles, prescriptions
- Dental, vision, and chiropractic
- Braces, LASIK, fertility, special schools
- OTC medications (by prescription)

Once the plan is in place, you can reimburse your employee for any medical expense they incur for themselves, their spouse, and their dependents.

- This includes any kind of health insurance, including major medical, long-term care (up to specific IRS limits), Medicare premiums, and even Medigap coverage.
- It includes copays, deductibles, "co-insurance," and other amounts insurance doesn't pay. That gets more important every year as insurance companies get better at nickel-and-diming you.

- It includes all your prescription drugs.

- It includes expenses for things like dental care, vision care, and chiropractic care that traditional insurance might not cover.

- It includes some really "big-ticket" items like braces for your kids' teeth, fertility treatments, and special schools for learning-disabled children. Let's say your physician diagnoses your 8-year-old son with ADHD, and prescribes *tai kwon* do lessons. Guess what—now those lessons are tax-deductible!

- It even includes over-the-counter medications and supplies, so long as they're actually prescribed by a physician.

One big advantage of the MERP is that it works with any insurance policy. You don't have to buy special coverage. You can use a MERP with insurance you buy on your own or insurance you buy through an exchange. If your spouse gets coverage from their employer, you can even set up a MERP in your business to cover whatever out-of-pocket expenses your spouse's insurance doesn't cover.

Let's assume you're a sole proprietor with two kids and you've hired your husband to work for your business. The plan lets you reimburse your husband/ employee for all medical and dental expenses he incurs for himself, his spouse (which brings you into the plan), and *his* dependents, your kids.

The best part is, this is money you'd spend anyway, whether you got a deduction or not. You'll spend your money on glasses or your kids' braces whether it's deductible or not. The MERP just lets you move it from someplace on your return where you certainly can't deduct all of it (and probably can't deduct *any* of it), to a place where you can.

The Paperwork

- Written plan document
- Benefits = "reasonable compensation"
- Document payments
- Certification
- PCORI fee

Okay, how do you make it work? Well, for starters, you'll need a written plan document. (We can help with that.)

If you've hired your spouse, you'll need to be able to verify that they qualify as a bona fide "employee." That means you need to direct the work they perform for the business, the same as you would direct the work that any other employee performs.

Here's one important requirement that the IRS *will* pay attention to in the unlikely event you get audited. You *do* have to run the payments through the actual business. You can't just pay medical bills out of the family personal account, total them up at the end of the year, and throw them on the business return.

This means you have two choices. You can pay health-care providers directly out of the business account. Or you can reimburse your employees for expenses they pay out of their personal funds. Let's say your husband needs to pick up a prescription. He can use his own money, and you can reimburse him. Or he can use a business credit card and charge it to the business directly.

There's generally no need for an outside third-party administrator, or "TPA," if you've simply hired your spouse to write off your own family's medical expenses. However, you will need a TPA if you're reimbursing nonfamily employees in order to avoid violating medical privacy rules.

There's no pre-funding required. You don't have to open a special bank or investment account, like with Health Savings Accounts or flex-spending plans. You don't have to decide up front how much you want to contribute to the plan, like you do with flexible spending accounts, and there's no "use it or lose it" rule. The MERP is really just an accounting device that lets you recharacterize your family medical bills as a business expense.

The MERP doesn't just help you save *income* tax. It also helps you save *self-employment* tax. Remember, when you work for yourself, you pay a special self-employment tax, which replaces the Social Security and Medicare taxes that you and your employer would share on your salary. That self-employment tax is based on your "net self-employment earnings"—but when you set up a MERP, the deduction reduces that self-employment income.

Employee Eligibility

Excludible Employees:

- Under age 25
- less than 35 hours/week
- less than 9 months/year
- less than 3 years service

Other Possible Excludible Employees:

- Controlled group rules
- Affiliated service groups

Here's the bad news. If you have non-family employees, you have to include them too. Now, you can exclude employees under age 25, who work less than 35 hours per week, less than nine months per year, or who have worked for you less than three years. You can also exclude employees covered by a collective bargaining agreement that includes health benefits. But still, having non-family employees may make it too expensive to reimburse everyone as generously as you'd cover your own family.

The Affordable Care Act now also imposes a pesky excise tax requirement on MERPs called the "Patient Centered Outcomes Research Trust Fund Fee," or PCORI fee. For plans operating in 2025, that amount is $3.47 per person, reported on IRS Form 720.

Yes, you heard that right. $3.47. You can't even buy a decent cup of coffee for that much. But the statutory penalty for failing to file that report can be as high as $10,000. And while it's not likely the IRS will ever actually impose that fine, you probably want to make sure you dot your "i's" and cross your "t's."

Health Savings Accounts

If a Medical Expense Reimbursement Plan isn't the right answer—either because you don't have a spouse to hire, or you have non-family employees you would have to cover— consider establishing a Health Savings Account (HSA). These arrangements combine a high-deductible health plan with a tax-free savings account to cover unreimbursed costs.

To qualify, you'll need to be covered by a "high deductible health plan." This means the deductible is at least $1,500 for single coverage or $3,000 for family coverage. Neither you nor your spouse can be covered by a "*non*-high deductible health plan" or by Medicare. The plan can't cover any expense, other than certain preventive care benefits, until you satisfy the annual deductible. You're not eligible if you're covered by a separate plan or rider offering prescription drug benefits before the minimum annual deductible is satisfied.

Once you've established your eligibility, you can open a deductible "health savings account" to cover out-of-pocket expenses not covered by your insurance. For 2025, you can contribute up to $4,300 if you have individual coverage or $8,550 if you have family coverage. (If you're 55 or older, you can save an extra $1,000 per year.)

HSAs are easy to open. Most banks, brokerage firms, and insurance companies offer them. Many accounts even offer a debit card to charge expenses directly to the account.

Once you're up and running, you can use your account for most kinds of health insurance, including

COBRA continuation and long-term care (but not "Medigap" coverage). You can also use it for the same sort of expenses as a MERP – copays, deductibles, prescriptions, and other out-of-pocket costs.

Withdrawals are tax-free so long as you use them for "qualified medical costs." Withdrawals *not* used for qualified medical costs are subject to regular income tax plus a 20% penalty.

Pay close attention to that last paragraph. Contributions are deductible, like a regular IRA (but not a Roth IRA). Withdrawals for qualified medical expenses are tax-free, like a Roth IRA (but not a regular IRA). That means the HSA is the *only* type of account in the entire tax code where you get a break on the money going in *and* the money coming out.

HSAs can be especially valuable if you plan on retiring before age 65, when Medicare kicks in. Retiring early means finding a way to pay for health insurance at the time in your life when it's as expensive as it can possibly be. Don't discount the value of socking away a tax-free war chest to cover that expense!

After your death, your account passes to your specified beneficiary. If your beneficiary is your spouse, they can treat it as their own HSA. If not, your beneficiary will pay ordinary tax on the account proceeds (but not the 20% penalty).

In some ways, the Health Savings Account isn't as powerful or flexible as the MERP. You've got specific dollar limits on what you can contribute to the account, which might not match your out-of-pocket costs. And there's no self- employment tax advantage as there is with a MERP. But Health Savings Accounts can still help cut your overall health-care costs by giving you bigger tax deductions than you might gain by merely deducting your out-of-pocket costs.

Flexible Spending Accounts

Flexible spending accounts ("FSAs") let you set aside pre- tax dollars for a variety of nontaxable fringe benefits, including health and disability insurance and medical expense reimbursement. Plan contributions avoid federal income and FICA tax.

The 2025 contribution limit for FSAs is $3,300. Before Obamacare, there were no contribution limits at all. Many observers have called the new $3,300 limit a tax in disguise, especially for older workers with expensive prescriptions who tend to stuff more into their accounts.

Once the money is in the account, you can use it for most medical expenses. However, nonprescription drugs and supplies, long-term care coverage, and associated expenses are not eligible FSA expenses.

Your employer deducts plan contributions from your paycheck and deposits them into your account until you claim your reimbursements.

When you enroll, you have to choose how much to contribute each pay period. You generally can't change your contribution amount in the middle of the plan year unless there's a change in your "family status." Eligible changes include marriage or divorce; birth, adoption, or death of a child; spousal employment; change in a dependent's student status; and the like.

You can claim your full year's reimbursement as soon as you incur qualifying expenses, whether you've fully funded your account for that amount or not.

Historically, FSA rules have required you to use your account balance by the end of the year or forfeit it. (That's why you see ads for prescription sunglasses in. December— to soak up FSA money.) However, many employers' plans have taken advantage of a subsequent ruling that lets them amend their plans to provide a 2½ month grace period immediately following the end of the year or allow up to $400 of carryover.

Missing a Home Office

Home office expenses are probably the most misunderstood deduction in the entire tax code. For years, taxpayers feared it guaranteed them an audit. Plenty of tax professionals were happy to go along with that myth. (Maybe they thought it made their jobs easier!) But the U.S. Supreme Court made it easier to qualify for the deduction back in 1994, and Congress made it even easier in 2007. So now your deduction is far less likely to attract attention.

Your home office is deductible if:

- It's your "principal place of business,"

- You use it to meet clients, patients, or prospects in the normal course of your trade or business, or

- It's a separate structure not attached to your dwelling unit.

Most deductible home offices qualify under Rule #1. IRS Publication 587 says your home office qualifies as your principal place of business if:

1. you use the space "exclusively and regularly for administrative or management activities of your trade or business," *and*

2. "you have no other fixed location where you conduct substantial administrative or management activities of your trade or business."

This is true even if you have another office, so long as you don't use it more than occasionally for administrative or management activities.

Example: You're a real estate agent and you have a desk at your broker's office. Your *home* office qualifies as your principal place of business so long as you use it to manage your business and keep your books, and you don't regularly do that at your desk at the broker.

Your home office doesn't have to be an entire room. You can use part of a room as long as it meets the requirements. You can also claim a workshop, a studio, or any other "separately identifiable" space you use to store products or samples. If you use it for more than one business, both have to qualify to take the deduction.

You have to use your office regularly and exclusively for business. "Regularly" generally means 10-12 hours per week. To prove your deduction, keep a log and take photos to record your business use.

Once you've qualified, you can start deducting expenses. If your business is taxed as a proprietorship, you'll use Form 8829. If you're taxed as a partnership or corporation, there's no separate form, which helps you "fly under the radar."

"Business Use Percentage"

2400

180

- Start by calculating the "business use percentage" of your home. You can divide by the number of rooms if they're roughly equal. Or you can calculate the exact percentage of the home's square footage the office occupies.

- Next, you'll deduct your business use percentage of your rent or your mortgage interest and property taxes. (Deducting those expenses on your business return can save you more than on your personal return. For example, if your state and local taxes are higher than $10,000, you'll sidestep that limit for the portion of property taxes attributable to the home office.

- You'll depreciate the business use percentage of your home's basis (excluding land) over 39 years as nonresidential property.

- Finally, you'll deduct your business use percentage of utilities, repairs, insurance, garbage pickup, and security.

Are there any other expenses you can allocate directly to your home office? Maybe you spent extra to renovate the room itself. Maybe you have especially high electric bills for home office equipment? You can claim those as "direct" expenses.

You can also deduct the cost of furnishing, carpeting, and decorating your home office. But be reasonable! If you buy a Picasso at auction, you don't get to deduct it just because it's in your office!

You can use home office expenses to reduce taxable income and self-employment income from your business, but not below zero. If your home office expenses in a particular year are more than your net income from your business, you can carry forward the loss to future years.

When you sell your home, you'll have to recapture any depreciation you claimed or could have claimed after May 6, 1997. You can still claim the usual $250,000 or $500,000 tax-free exclusion for space you use for your office unless it's a "separate dwelling unit."

If this all seems like too much work, there's a newer "safe harbor" method that lets you claim a flat $5 per square foot (regardless of your actual expenses) for up to 300 square feet of qualifying home office space (regardless of what percentage it occupies in your home). If you use the safe harbor, you'll continue to deduct your mortgage interest and property tax on Schedule A. However, you'll forego any depreciation deduction. And if the safe harbor deduction reduces your business income below zero, there's no carrying forward the loss.

The safe harbor is certainly easier than the traditional method. However, using it might not let you claim nearly as much as the traditional method. The only way to know for sure is to run the numbers and calculate the deduction both ways.

Claiming a home office can also boost your car and truck deductions. That's because it can minimize or even eliminate nondeductible commuting miles for that business.

Example: You're a real estate agent with a desk at your broker's office. If you don't have a home office, your trip from home to the office is a nondeductible commute. However, if you have a home office, and you start your workday in that office, your "commute" is the trip to the home office, and your trip from home to your desk at the broker is a deductible trip from one business location to another.

Missing Car & Truck Expenses

Now let's talk about the most common mistake that business owners and professionals make with vehicle expenses— specifically, calculating them the wrong way.

You know that you can calculate your "actual expenses" for operating your vehicle. Or you can use a much easier standard allowance. For 2025, the allowance is 70 cents per mile. Sounds pretty good, right? Well, it might surprise you to see how much it *really* costs to operate your car. And it's almost *never* 70 cents per mile!

Every year, AAA researches vehicle operating costs. As the 2021 table shows, if you're taking the standard deduction for a car that costs you more than 70 cents/mile, you're losing money every time you turn the key.

AAA Driving Costs	
Vehicle	Cents/Mile
Small Sedan	50.1
Medium Sedan	58.2
Large Sedan	74.6
Medium 4WD SUV	67.3
Minivan	66.9

Your first step involves calculating your "business use percentage" (BUP) for your vehicle. The IRS divides your trips into three categories: 1) business; 2) commuting; and 3) personal. Ordinary commuting and personal trips are nondeductible. Trips from home to your first business stop and trips from your last business stop to home are personal. (Daily trips to the bank, post office, and similar stops where you perform no service don't qualify as "business.")

Oh, and because you'll ask, yes, you can deduct the cost of plastering your name and logo on your vehicle.

But the IRS specifically says that "wrapping" your car won't convert personal or commuting miles into deductible business miles. Sorry!

Now that we know what qualifies as "business" miles, the IRS gives you four ways to track them. All four require you to keep "adequate records or other sufficient evidence" to support your business use. This means logging mileage at least weekly and keeping receipts for all expenses over $75.

- **"Brute Force" method:** Record every business mile you drive for the year. Divide your business mileage by your total mileage for the year to calculate BUP. (If you use more than one car for business, this is the method you have to use. We know, what a hassle.)

- **"90 days" method:** Record your business miles for a "typical" 90-day period. Divide that amount by your total mileage for that period to calculate BUP, then use that percentage for the entire year.

- **"First Week" method:** Record your business miles for the first week each month. Divide that by your total miles for that period and use it for the entire month.

- **"Simplified" method:** Record your starting and ending mileage for a 90-day period. Record your personal and commuting miles for that period, and assume all the *rest* of your miles are for business. Calculate your BUP and use it for the entire year. (This is the easiest method if most of your miles are for business.)

Travel between temporary business stops is deductible. So, for example, if you leave home, make six business stops, meet a prospect for dinner, then drive home, your mileage between your first stop and the restaurant is deductible. However, if you have a regular business stop (one that you make at least 8 to 10 times in a six-month period) that you expect to last less than a year, you can count those as business miles, too. If home is your principal place of business, then all business trips are deductible.

Once you've calculated your BUP, you have two ways to calculate your deduction.

1. The **mileage allowance**, which is the flat 70 cents/mile for 2025, *plus* parking, tolls, and your BUP of interest on your car loan and state and local personal property tax on the vehicle.

2. The **"actual expense"** method, where you deduct your full BUP of all expenses. These include:

   - Depreciation and interest (if you've bought),
   - Lease payments (if you've leased),
   - Insurance,
   - Gas, oil changes, and car washes,
   - Tires, maintenance, repairs,
   - License and registration fees,
   - Personal property tax payments, and
   - Parking and tolls.

Which one saves the most? Easy—try them both and see. Generally, the more you drive, the more the allowance saves. That's because the allowance assumes 14 cents/mile for depreciation – and as your miles climb, that "assumed" amount can be far more than your actual depreciation. If you're a real road warrior, logging 30,000 or more business miles per year, you'll almost certainly come out ahead with the allowance, no matter what you drive.

Okay. What if you've been taking the mileage allowance (because it's easier, or because your tax preparer told you it was all the same), and you discover you ought to be taking actual expenses. What now? Well, if you're taking the allowance now, you *can* switch to the "actual expense" method *if* you own your car, but *not* if you lease.

Unfortunately, the reverse isn't true. You can't switch from actual expenses to the mileage allowance. You also can't use the allowance if you use five or more vehicles in your business, or you use your vehicle for hire (taxi, Lyft, Uber, etc.).

Missing Meals and Entertainment

Now let's take a minute to discuss some fun deductions for business meals.

The concept here is that you can deduct the cost of meals you host with a bona fide business purpose. This means conversations with clients, prospects, referral sources, and business colleagues. And let me ask you – when do you ever eat with someone who's *not* a client, prospect, referral source, or business colleague? If you're in a field like real estate, insurance, or investments, where you're constantly marketing "the brand called you," the answer might be "never." Be as inclusive as you can with what you define as bona fide business discussion!

The general rule now is, that you can deduct 100% of your meals, so long as they aren't "lavish or extraordinary." You can deduct the cost of food, drinks, taxes, and tips. (Yes, that includes the coat check and valet parker.)

You generally can't deduct the cost of meals you eat with your spouse unless you're traveling together for business. However, you can include the cost of a spouse or other "closely connected" person if your guest brings *their* spouse.

Documenting expenses is probably easier than you think. You don't need receipts for expenses under $75. But you do need to record five pieces of information in your business diary or records. (Credit card statements work for the first three as long as you corroborate them with the fourth and fifth in some sort of diary or log):

1. How much you spent

2. When you spent it

3. Where you spent it

4. Your business relationship with your guest (prospect, client, referral source, vendor, etc.)

5. The business purpose of the meal

Do you entertain at home? Do you ever discuss business when you do? (Of course.) Are you deducting those meals, too? (Probably not.) There's no requirement that you have to eat out to deduct the costs of a meal. So don't forget to deduct home entertainment expenses too! If you invite up to a dozen guests, use the same rules as if you were eating out. If you invite more than 12 guests, you can deduct "reasonable" costs if your primary purpose is business. Include employees; let guests know your business purpose; discuss and display your product or service to support your deduction.

You can also deduct off-premises meals you provide as part of required business meetings.

You can also deduct 100% of your expenses for meals and entertainment for sales seminars and similar events where the meal is integral to the presentation or the business. (If you're a Somali pirate, for example, you can deduct 100% of the cost of meals you provide to crews you hold hostage on your ship.)

Now here's some bad news. It used to be that you could also deduct entertainment expenses for events like ball games, movies, or concerts, if they took place directly before or after substantial, bona fide discussion directly related to the active conduct of your business. You could deduct the face value of tickets to events, food and drinks, parking, taxes, and tips.

At least, you *could.* The Tax Cuts and Jobs Act of 2017 eliminates that deduction.

While we're on the topic of hospitality, let's talk about business gifts. Gifts you give to business associates are deductible up to $25 if you can show a business purpose for the expense or business benefit to be gained. (Married couples count as one person for this rule—you can't deduct $25 for each.) This includes your family and friends if they qualify as bona fide clients, prospects, or referral sources. Gifts are nontaxable to the recipient.

- If you give a gift to a group of recipients, such as a family or an office, you can deduct $25 for each member of the group.
- Advertising specialties like pens and other tchotchkes with a value up to $4 each are deductible as advertising expenses and don't count against the $25 per person annual limit for business gifts. Contest prizes you give to customers (but not employees) also qualify.

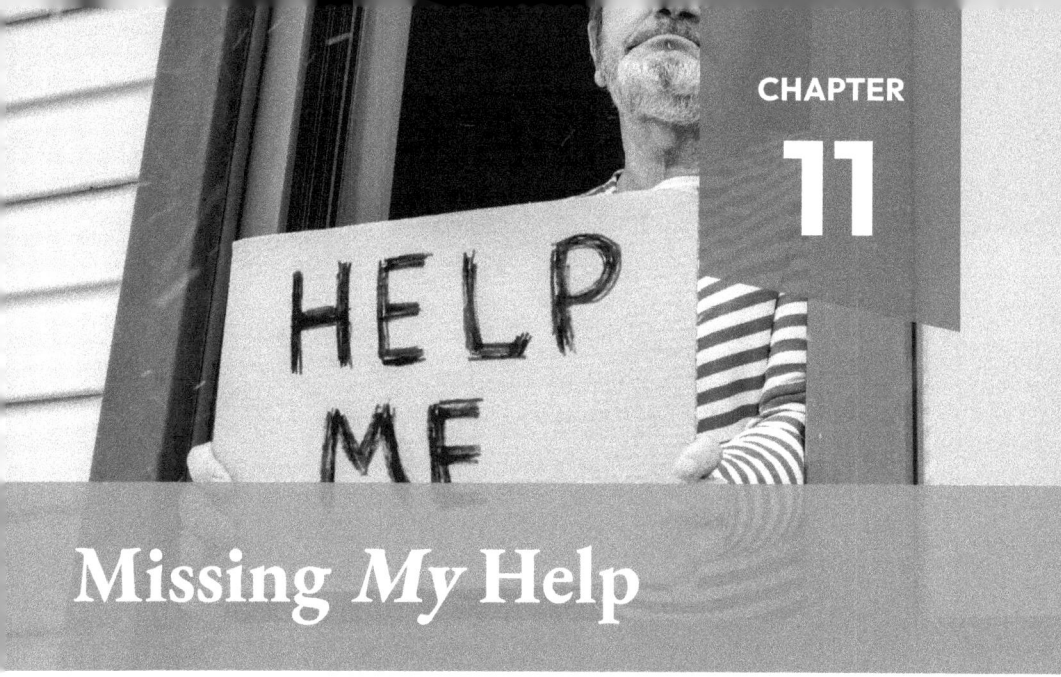

Missing *My* Help

Now that you see how business owners miss out on tax breaks, let's talk about the final mistake. And that is (drumroll, please) failing to take advantage of *my* help.

Way back in Chapter One, we talked about how most tax professionals drive using the rearview mirror. They do a perfectly decent job recording the history *you* give them – but they don't do much, if anything, to help you write a new history – one that costs you less in the taxes we all hate to pay.

In the course of reading this book, you've probably found some things you aren't doing as effectively as you could be. Maybe you're operating your business in the wrong entity. Maybe you're missing a home office deduction you really deserve. Maybe you're missing out on car and truck deductions, or meals and entertainment.

And you probably haven't done *any* real *planning* at all. (That's OK—most of my clients haven't, simply because they don't realize how important it really is.)

If that's the case, then isn't it about time you stop driving in the rearview mirror? Isn't it time you stop settling for just recording history?

That's where *I* come in.

I give you the plan you need to stop wasting thousands of dollars in tax you don't have to pay.

How does it work? Excel Empire's tax planning process works the same as if you see a doctor because you aren't feeling well.

First, the doctor arrives at a diagnosis. Let's say your stomach hurts. Did you get some bad blue cheese last night? Maybe it's just food poisoning. Is it something more serious like gastritis? Or is it contagious death cancer, and time to start getting your affairs in order?

Regardless of what the problem is, the first step is identifying it.

Next, the doctor prescribes some sort of solution. Maybe it's medication. Maybe it's surgery. Maybe it's physical therapy. Maybe it's time and bed rest . . . but in most cases, it'll be something. The problem won't just solve itself.

Finally, someone has to fill that prescription This is where you see the real results. If you don't fill the prescription, you won't feel better.

Our process starts with a Discovery Call. We'll ask a series of questions about your income and expenses, assets and liabilities, and financial goals. Then we'll gather your tax returns and supporting documents to spot the potential green lights that haven't yet found their way to your returns.

Next, our team of tax planners analyzes those documents and identifies how much we can save you. This isn't just an estimate, it's a guarantee. We'll schedule a call where we present our letter of engagement to deliver your prescription.

Our fees will always be less than your first-year savings. And if you don't actually realize those savings, we'll refund as much of that fee as we fall short of that guarantee. If we promise you $100,000 of savings, and we miss that mark by $20,000, we'll refund 20% of your fee. You literally cannot lose.

Finally, our affiliated CPA firm works with you to fill your prescriptions. We've assembled a complete team of nationally recognized experts to help you in specialty areas like risk management, business and real estate sales, charitable and estate planning, and special purpose business entities.

You'll be satisfied knowing you're doing everything the law allows to get that tax bill off your back. And you'll rest easy knowing everything we recommend is court-tested and IRS- approved.

I can't promise how much you'll save until we sit down with you and your returns. But I can promise you'll save more than if you keep driving with the rearview mirror!

So please, call me with your questions. Come to me for a *plan*. You have nothing to lose but taxes, and possibly thousands to gain. Why would you wait to make that call?

Questions and Notes

Questions and Notes

Questions and Notes

Questions and Notes

....

....

....

....

....

....

....

....

....

....

....

....

....

....